MEMOIRS:

I0171057

A BROKEN SOUL

.

KELLY TROTMAN

MEMOIRS: A BROKEN SOUL

Printed in the United States of America

ISBN-13:978-0692264447

ISBN-10:0692264442

Printed by Createspace in 2014

Published by BlaqRayn Publishing in 2014

Dedications

First and foremost I would like to thank my Lord and Savior Jesus Christ for without him none of this would be possible. Thank you for blessing me with the love of reading, writing and the gift of poetry!

To my sons Justin and Joe'l you are my inspiration and my motivation. Everything that I do is for you'll. The two of you'll are my everything and the reason that I work so hard. I want you'll to know that you can do and become anything that you want to as long as you have faith and you work hard. I'm extremely proud of you'll and so lucky to have you'll call me mom!

To my mother Peggy Trotman thank you for buying me and endless supply of books as a kid and for always encouraging me to do what I love no matter what. I love you very much!

To my big sister Tesha for as long as I can remember you have motivated me and encouraged me to write. Thank you for believing in me when even I didn't

believe in myself I love you to no end
sissy!

To my brother in law Tyrone thank you
for always having my back and keeping
me on my toes you're truly one of a
kind love you always!

To my Nephew Ken-dell I'm so proud of
you keep up the great work, stay
focused and never give up on your
dreams love you!

To my niece Jada you're blossoming
into a beautiful, smart and talented
young woman. I am so proud of you
keep your head up stay focused you're
destined for greatness! I love you!

To my friends/family/supporters Carol
Bradley, Tonelle Lawrence , Jackie
Gray, Quarran Perkins, NeNe Capri,
Cash Streetlit Author, Denise Brooks,
Zoleka Reid , Kim Morrow, Stephanie
White, Cassandra Cromer, Shawnda
Hamilton, Qytisah Stokes, Anel Adams,
Dr. Ariz Mehta, Tynifah, Lakeisha
Holmes, Conya Thorpe, Lisa Moore,
Kenya Anthony. Thank you'll for the
motivation, encouragement, listening
ears. You'll have contributed in one

way or another to helping me on my journey and I truly appreciate it. I love you'll!

Last but not least to the readers I really hope you enjoy this book . It's filled with some of my deepest thoughts and true life experience's letting them out and putting them on paper has really helped me and hopefully it will help someone else out there as well.

Peace and Blessings Kelly!

MEMOIRS:

A BROKEN SOUL

KELLY TROTMAN

Girl Gone Wild!!

Tired of the lies tired of stress tired

of bullshit when will it rest.

Everyday it's something new call me

telling me about shit you

Didn't do. Why do you feel you need

to impress you lie about your

Looks and how you dress. You sleep

with different men all the time

You say you get money but you

never have a dime. You don't even

Know the identity of the father of

your child that's what happens when

a

Girl goes wild. You talk about your

friend's family too stab them in the

back

Use them and you're through. But

when you're gone you're never far

away

Because no matter how hard you try

nothing goes your way. You always

Get burned you always get used and

then you want to turn to the people

You've bruised but no one is there to

dry your tears you've hurt to many

People over the years so now you're

alone with all your dirt now you

know

How it feels to hurt maybe now

you'll grow up stop acting like a child

this

Is what happens when a girl goes

wild!!!

A Child's Pain!

Stressed compressed years of pain and suffering began to rain.

In my head complete despair thinking that this life is so unfair up

And down my emotions go steaming heat from head to toe

Aggravation anger the epitome of joy being strung like a yo-yo

A selfless toy. Why should a child have to go through this a temporary?

Roof a temporary bed not knowing

where to lay her head. Today here

Tomorrow there now tell me if you

think this life is fair!

Someday!

As I sit in my room alone looking around
I wonder will true love ever be found. I
know one day my prince will appear
but will he be a frog in disguise I fear. I
want someone who will love me and
treat me right and when it's late and
I'm asleep he holds me tight. I don't
know when I don't know where but by
the will of God I know someday my
prince will be here.

The Meaning of Love!

Love means nice

Love means sweet

It makes you strong

And at the same time makes you weak!

Love is a kiss

Love is a hug

Love is hey boo or hey snuggle bug love
means

Happiness love means truth

So if love means all of these things why

don't I

Love you?

Him!

Crazy emotions elicit thoughts visions of happiness right from the start.

Who is this person who captures my soul who knew I'd let my guard down not half this time but as a whole. He makes me want to plan for the future which is something I just don't do. But with this man my heart is open. Could this be my come true? I'm nervous and excited at the same time counting down the days that he'll be mine!!

Definition of Him!

His walk his talk his laugh his smile are

all the things that make him

worthwhile. His wit his charm his soul

are all the things that make him whole.

His love his pain his joy his fame loving

kind genuine and sweet are all the

things that swept me off of my feet!

Get it together!

Still playing games still haven't learned yet I'm here to tell you your match you've met! Sitting in the house can't pick up the phone but if I don't call your ass you whine moan and groan. What the fuck do you think this is a game? Like I'm supposed to sit in the house like some kind of lame? Sitting by the phone I just can't do! What you won't another man will gladly do for you! I'm not going to pretend that I don't care but when I need you you're just simply not there. Is this the way you want it to be I go my way and let

you be free? If this is what you really
want then be a man no need to front
speak your mind just be upfront
because right now we're wasting time.
I told you to go then I took you back
but when it comes to love there are
things you still lack. Love me please me
or leave me alone because when I go
this time trust me I'm gone! No turning
back so if you truly love me nigga pick
up the fucking slack!

Why?

Why do men lie and swear that the love
for another man is just not there. Why
is it in the daytime they're kissing on
she but late in the night they're
grinding with he. Why not be open why
not come clean, why come sleep with
me and still continue to be a part of
the down low scene? Why get married
with a child and a home if every time
you turn around you have to whisper on
the phone. Whisper to a man who is
supposed to be your boy but you'll are
sitting on the phone reminiscing about
a toy, a toy he used to make you moan

& groan and after that you brought

your trifling ass home a poker game a

club is where you say you went but we

both know with a man is where your

night was spent!

My Child!

An angel delicate sweet kind hearted
and wild these are the words that
describe my child. Loving caring a heart
of gold. I hope he keeps these qualities
when he gets old. Smart, funny,
courageous full of potential and success,
as a man of God I know he will truly
grow to be the best!

To whom it may concern

To Whom It May Concern today is the
day I thought I would be happy in every
way. The day when I would say I do the
day when he would say it too but
unfortunately that's not it how goes he
didn't say I do or even hello he didn't
say I love you and yes I still care or
even tell me he'd always be there. He
didn't ask if I was alright. He couldn't
even come and say goodnight! Is this
the man I say I love who doesn't show
affection or any type of love. Can
anybody tell me what went wrong? Did I
go to fast or wait too long? How will all

this end you'd say? I guess we'll have to wait for another day. To whom it may concern!

This Morning

I woke up with love on my mind with the thought in my head of the man I would find. What kind of man do you want my friend said? The kind of man that comes home because he loves me not just to go to bed. One who says I love you and I know it's true, one that says your number one there's no one above you! One who will hold me through the night and in my heart I know it's right! This is what I want I hope you understand. What I really want is a man who's a man!

Let Go!

Holding on to stress, pain from the past
is an easy way to make sure your
newfound happiness doesn't last.
People always say let it go and just
move on but if it was that simple this
headache would have been long gone!
I've tried to forget and I've tried to
forgive but the hurt in my heart deep
within still lives. I know it's unhealthy
to hold on to the pain but every time I
open my heart it seems that nothing
has changed. They say I'll never leave,
I'll always be true but as quick as it's
said they're on to someone new! How

can I believe, how can I dream when every time I fall in love I get the same thing? Lies, cheating, hurt and pain and when I try to leave he says babe I'll change. I know it's out there I know true love exist but I won't find it until I let go of this!

Am I?

Am I really insane or will things ever

change? Are my feelings in my head? I

don't even dream when I go to bed! Is

there something wrong I say to feel this

way every day?

Am I really insane to be in love and still

feel pain? Does my man really care

what's in his heart is there love still

there or does he pretend to really care?

I love you boo is what he says , is this

real or is this fake will this love last or

will my heart break? To lose this man

would be a shame but I'd rather feel

love instead of pain!

You!

I smile when I hear you talk on the phone. I melt when hear your sexy voice moan. When you told me you loved me it knocked me off my feet. A better love I just could not meet! We fight, we yell, we argue and swear but always know that my heart will be there. Everyone has ups and downs but where there's true love you and I can be found!

Alone!

Away from home and all alone no friends no family to call my own. Hurt, lonely, confused out of whack, depressed cold afraid to look back. What will they say how will they feel will everything be ok or just a big deal? They told me not to go they told me to stay but their loving advice I just didn't obey. So here I am alone and confused feeling nothing but abandoned and used!

One Day

One day happiness will appear but I

have the feeling that you won't be near.

I give you my all I've always been true

but at the end of the day that just

doesn't seem to be enough for you.

Honesty, loyalty faithfulness is what

you claim you want but when it's given

to you I think that it's all a front. I've

opened my heart and bared my soul but

the more love I give you the more yours

seems to be on hold. Do I run? Do I stay?

Do I fight for what I want or just leave

you alone? Move on with my life and let

go and allow my heart to once again

close?

What Goes Around Comes Around!!!

Sitting in my room thinking of how to fill this void I need you I want you but I can't be your toy having you in my life made me feel complete but little did I know that down the road my heart would meet defeat I was faithful, committed and true to only you three little things that you just couldn't seem to do.

You told me your heart was reserved only for me but as I looked deeper in your eyes the love I just couldn't see

you constantly told me how much you
loved me and how you would never put
anyone above me an as soon as I began
to let my guard down to the arms of
another women is where you were
found so tell me how deep was your
love from the start.

I gave you my time and my heart but it
seems the more I gave the more you
tore me apart loving you made me feel
like I was drowning inside when you
told me you stop loving me I thought
my heart had died I can't believe for
months you sat there and lied and
covered your dirt while I sat in my

room alone with my hurt but it's cool

I'm over that now but I want you to

know when there's love you've found

remember the quote what goes around

comes around!!

Thirsty

Baby I'm thirsty for you

I am so thirsty for

You it feels like sand

Is blowing through my body

I feel like I opened my

Mouth and the desert flew

In.

I don't know who invented

The word break-up but

Whoever did they obviously

Didn't know you your truly one

Of a kind and I love you.

Pissed!

Yesterday I was happy today I'm pissed every fucking day this nigga takes me through shit why I ask do you stress me out when every time I turn around it's love you talk about how do you love me when you treat me like shit tell me would you feel better if I cut off your dick.

You say you're my husband and I'm your wife but when exactly do I fit in your life..you laugh at me when I express my gripe but how funny would it be if I went and got a knife would you think it's a joke would you think it's for fun would your stupid ass stand there or would you run take heed to it ignore it do as you choose but if you keep fucking with me for sure you will lose!!!

Five Days

So it's been five days and still no calls I
guess he doesn't love me after all I
tried to deny it pretend it wasn't true
when the signs were in my face clear as
the morning dew I try to block him out
of my mind but the harder I try the
more I find that my love for him cannot
be denied let it go let it go is what they
say but I know if it was them they
would fight to stay.

Young Love!

All this time I thought I was in control
but in one quick moment he captured
my sole his smart mouth and feisty
ways had me loving this boy in only 2
days his presence his voice gives me
such joy damn how I am in love with
this young ass boy he's too young is
what people say but who the hell are
you to judge my relationship this way I
love him now and will tomorrow and if
you can't understand that then for you
I feel sorrow!

Deep Within

I knew that one day this man would arrive didn't know the month, year day or the time. I knew you would be the one to stop my heart from always being on the run. From all of the fake love, empty promises, and relationship based on fun.you complete me, you fill me you make my heart sing my feelings awaken with every touch that you bring.

Your words embrace my soul they fill me from inside out making me whole. I pray and hope our time together doesn't end because you're the first to

really touch me within!

Happiness Begins Within

So many wait for happiness to come from the hands of someone else not knowing that happiness from inside is the first way that it should be felt. No one thing can bring you pure joy not money not fame not even affection from a girl or boy to be completely happy you must find it within yourself because if you keep looking outward it will never be felt!

True success!

Success comes in many forms I'll never think less of mines because it doesn't compare to yours.

Success is accomplishing goals, dreams and tasks to make your life improve my success depends on me not on how you do what you do money ,fame and popularity yeah it all sounds good but what use is it if having all of that hasn't added to your life so you could internally improve?

So do things your way and do them for

you or when you finally reach success

you'll still have a lot to prove!

Stay in your lane!

Stay in your lane run your own race
stop trying to be like next keep your
own pace. Trying to compete with the
next person wastes nothing but time
because while you'll watching them
you're not making a dime everyone else
is living making their dreams come true
but resentment and bitterness is all
that surrounds you live your life if you
want things to change focus on your life
instead of swerving into someone else's
lane!

About The Author

Kelly Trotman is a native of Newark, NJ and mother of two boys that are every beat of her heart. Against all odds and all those who told her that she wouldn't amount to anything has consistently proved everyone wrong!

Kelly has become a certified phlebotomist, obtained a degree in culinary arts, CEO of Kelly's Catering and founded a very successful promotions company called EyeLuv Books Promotions.

She is currently pursuing her bachelor's degree in business and entrepreneurship proudly making liars out of the naysayers and doubters who swore that she would never be successful.

Today she's an aspiring author her debut novel memoirs a broken soul will bring you face to face with love, heartache, laughter, pain and joy. Through her hard work and accomplishment's she has learned that a bumpy road makes the success even sweeter!

Kelly Trotman